Third Eye Awakening

The Third Eye, techniques to open the third eye, how to enhance psychic abilities, and much more!

Table of Contents

Introduction 3

Chapter 1: What Is The Third Eye 4

Chapter 2: History Of The Third Eye 6

Chapter 3: The Different Psychic Abilities 8

Chapter 4: What It Means To Open The Third Eye 13

Chapter 5: Techniques For Opening The Third Eye 15

Chapter 6: Chakras & The Third Eye 20

Chapter 7: Using Crystals With Your Third Eye 27

Chapter 8: Ways To Sharpen Your Psychic Abilities 29

Chapter 9: Third Eye Awakening With Meditation 36

Chapter 10: Third Eye Awakening With Health & Diet 38

Chapter 11: The Pineal Gland & DMT 40

Chapter 12: How To Avoid Pineal Gland Calcification 43

Chapter 13: The Third Eye & Brainwave Levels 45

Conclusion 47

Introduction

Thank you for taking the time to pick up this book: Third Eye Awakening.

This book covers the topic of third eye awakening, what it is, and how to ultimately open your third eye. You will soon learn about the third eye in different cultures, the beliefs that surround it, and also what we know about it scientifically.

At the completion of this book you will have a good understanding of your third eye and will be well equipped with some tactics and strategies to open and awaken it. You will soon discover about the different psychic abilities that can be developed when the third eye is awakened, and also some strategies for how to train and improve them further.

Awakening the third eye is absolutely key to spiritual enlightenment, developing psychic abilities, and finding clarity in your life.

Embark on an incredible journey today by learning more about your third eye, and how to finally awaken it!

Once again, thanks for taking the time to read this book, I hope you find it to be helpful, and wish you the best of luck on your journey!

Chapter 1:
What Is The Third Eye

So, what exactly is the third eye?

The third eye is essentially a 'hidden' eye, said to be situated between your brows. It makes mention is several religions and spiritual traditions, and is said to possess certain powers.

These powers allow people to have psychic-type experiences, where they may connect with a spiritual entity, communicate with a spirit guide, have some sort of out of body experience, or experience a range of other unusual occurrences.

The Pineal gland is often associated with the third eye. The pineal gland is an endocrine gland located in the vertebrate brain. This gland is also located between the two brows, and excretes melatonin which regulates our sleeping patterns.

The Pineal gland gets mentioned in several spiritual traditions, yet there is no scientific or medically proven connection that this gland provides a 6th sense.

When you have a 'hunch' and then act upon it, it is said that you are using your third eye. Though it can be much further refined and developed and used for a lot more than simple intuition.

To break it down further, the third eye is said to allow us to 'see' or 'visualize' energy. This energy could be in the form of something in the past, a vision of the future, communication with a spirit or entity, sensing that something has/will happen, and more.

However, in today's age most people aren't in-tune with their third eye. It is said to be closed or asleep. This is where awakening the third eye comes into play. To make full use of your third eye, you must awaken it and open it – which is the primary topic of this book.

In the following chapters you will learn more about the third eye, the different abilities it can provide you with, the dangers and myths surrounding it, and of course – how to awaken, open, and use your third eye!

Despite the common misconception, absolutely anyone can open and make use of their third eye. People may have varying natural abilities and potential for using their third eye, but it is something that everybody can further develop.

Read on to discover a bit of the history of the third eye, and it's role in different religions and spiritual practices!

Chapter 2:
History Of The Third Eye

The third eye (also known as the inner eye) is the concept of an invisible eye that provides a person with perception beyond ordinary sight.

This third eye is mentioned in many old texts and even today in modern religious traditions and spiritual practices.

The third eye is mentioned in Hinduism, Taoism, and also in Theosophy, among other practices and belief systems.

Each religion or philosophy has its own beliefs and opinions regarding the third eye, what is does, and how it works.

Hinduism

In Hinduism the third eye refers to the 'ajna' or 'brow chakra'. Chakras are discussed in more depth later on in this book, but essentially chakras are energy points. The third eye is said to be the 6th primary chakra, or energy point in the body. According to Hindu tradition, it is a part of the brain that can be made stronger through repetition – just like a muscle.

Like mentioned in the previous chapter, anyone can improve their skills and abilities that their third eye unlocks. The Hindu belief of being able to strengthen the third eye coincides with that fact.

In Hinduism, it is believed that the third eye is connected with our intuition, and allows people to do things such as see the future or sense things.

Taoism

Taoism, and many other Chinese religious sects, also teach that the third eye is located between the brows. They believe that by meditating and focusing on the vibrations in the third eye area, that people are able to reach extremely deep levels of meditation.

According to Taoism, the third eye is one of the main 'energy centers' of the body, and can only be opened in a deep state of meditation.

Theosophy

Some Theosophists believe that the third eye is actually a partially dormant pineal gland. Some believe that through training, this third eye can be developed to allow telescopic and microscopic vision.

Chapter 3:
The Different Psychic Abilities

In this chapter we will be discussing some of the different psychic abilities that people possess, and that can be honed and improved through opening the third eye.

Some people naturally have some of these abilities, whereas others do not. Some will also find it easier to develop certain abilities over others. What your natural propensity for each of these abilities is will vary from everyone else, and you will only discover which of these abilities you are most gifted with through practice.

Clairvoyance

A clairvoyant is a person who can clearly see non-physical realities and entities. These people can often view auras, energies, spirits, and different entities.

Clairaudience

Clairaudience is the ability to hear events occurring in another place, or even in another dimension. It is similar to clairvoyance, but instead of actually seeing the energies, spirits, activities, and entities – clairaudients hear them.

Clairsensitivity

A person who is clairsensitive can feel surrounding energies, spirits, and activities. This may come as a physical sensation, or as an overwhelm of a particular emotion. Many clairsensitive people also get these messages through the sense of smell.

Remote-Viewing

Remote viewing is also sometimes referred to as travelling clairvoyance. A remote viewer can see things happening in another location, be it physical or not. Often this occurs in real-time, with their eyes open.

Astral Travel

Astral travel is the ability to travel along the astral plane, to another location. This occurs during sleep. Normally, this involves the astral traveler visualizing themselves leaving their physical body, attached by a long cord. From here, astral travelers are free to roam wherever they wish, communicate with other entities, and visit other places – be them physically real or not. People have been said to astral travel to locations, and gleam information that proved to be 100% correct in reality. Some astral travelers also use their skills to communicate with other people and entities during their travels.

Lucid Dreamer

A lucid dreamer is somebody who can control their dreams. A lot of people naturally have this ability when they are young, but lose it over time. It can however, be developed and worked upon. This is related to astral projection, and many people learn to become lucid dreamers before stepping into the world of astral travel.

Pre-cognition

Pre-cognition is the ability to gather information from the future. This information is not always correct, as future events can be changed based on the pre-cognitor's actions.

Retro-Cognition

Retro-cognition is the ability to gather information from the past. This can also mean information gathered from the past in a non-physical dimension. This can come in the form of visions of the past, certain emotions, voices, smells and a general sense of an event occurring.

Telepathy

Telepathy is the ability to communicate from mind-to-mind. It is the ability to send messages, simply via thought to another human. Some advanced telepaths are able to send and receive very clear messages to one another. Most people have experienced some level of telepathy before. A common occurrence is thinking strong thoughts about another person, and then all of a sudden, that person rings them.

Psychography

A psychographer is a person who does automatic writing, or psychic writing. Another energy or entity takes control of what the person writes, and they often subconsciously are able to communicate messages through writing or drawing. The psycographer simply dictates, either consciously or subconsciously.

Medium

A medium is a person who brings information from the non-physical dimension, to the physical dimension. They 'mediate' the information. Everyone has a certain level of medium ability. Mediums can work in a variety of ways, from telepathy, to psychography, to having visions that they relay.

Psychophoning

Psychophoning is when a non-physical consciousness or entity uses your physical body to speak. This can happen both consciously and subconsciously. This can be a frightening phenomenon for many, as the medium may not be in control of the experience.

Psychic Healing

Psychic healing is the ability to use energy to heal yourself or another person. The psychic healer uses intense focus to direct healing energy to the person with an ailment, either in person or from a distance. It requires intense visualization and focus to achieve, but has existed in many forms throughout history – such as Reiki healing.

Aural Viewing

Aural viewing is the ability to view another person's aura. An aura is an energy field of colors that surround a person's body. It can be viewed both in person and also through photographs. The different colors of an aura indicate a person's emotions and energy that they are emitting. It can point to different health problems, and also provide an indication of a person's true character.

Telekinesis

Telekinesis is the ability to move objects with your mind. You may have seen people who can bend spoons with their mind – that is an example of this ability!

In Conclusion

Those are a few of the most common psychic abilities that people possess and can develop. You may have a natural propensity for some of them, and might struggle to develop others. Each person is individual in that regard. You may have even experienced some of these abilities in your own life previously.

In order to improve and develop these abilities in yourself, you must first become in-tune with your body and awaken your third eye.

Chapter 4:
What It Means To Open The Third Eye

So what does it mean to 'open' the third eye?

Firstly, you need to understand that for most people, the third eye lies dormant. The third eye, or sixth chakra is said to be the key to a person's psychic potential and has the ability to unlock a whole different world for those that can release it's potential.

We use words such as 'open' or 'awaken' when talking about activating the third eye and its power because it does lie dormant in most.

When we open our third eye, we are making use of the potential, and power of the third eye. We are consciously diverting our attention to the third eye, and allowing ourselves to use its power.

Because the majority of us allow the third eye to lie dormant for so long, it can become tough to open it back up. You almost have to re-train your body and mind to be able to access its power. You must also ensure that all of your chakras or energy pathways are clear and that there are no emotional or physical issues that are blocking your energy, or chi, from reaching the third eye.

Once the third eye is awakened, you will be able to finally tap into some of its power. This of course will take practice and time to learn. Also, as you continue, the power of your third eye will often increase, and that combined with practicing your abilities will allow you to achieve an extreme level of consciousness and intuition.

Some believe that the reason that the third eye lies dormant is because the pineal gland has become calcified. Diet, meditation, and some other techniques can be used to de-calcify the pineal gland and awaken the third eye!

In the next chapter, we will discuss some techniques for awakening and opening your third eye!

Chapter 5:
Techniques For Opening The Third Eye

As mentioned in the previous chapter, for the majority of you reading this, your third eye has been lying dormant for many years and your pineal gland has calcified.

Usually, opening the third eye is not a rapid process, and will take a mixture of techniques over a period of time.

This chapter will provide a few options for ways to awaken your third eye, originating from different belief systems all over the world. One method may be enough for you, but for most people it is best to combine a mixture of them to achieve the desired result!

Avoid Fluoride

Fluoride can be a cause for the pineal gland to become calcified. Fluoride is in tap water, toothpaste, some fruits and vegetables, and in some processed meat! Make sure that you use a water filter, and try and consume organic, fluoride-free foods.

This can be quite tough to do at first and it may take your body a while to adapt to the change. Gradually, it will become easier, and you should begin to feel more in-tune with your body!

Use a Detoxifier or Supplement

Using a supplement to detoxify your pineal gland can be extremely helpful in improving the condition of your Pineal gland and awakening your third eye. Some of the best supplements and ingredients to begin using are: Hydrilla verticillata, chlorella, spirulina, blue-green algae, Iodine, zeolite, ginseng, borax, D3, bentonite clay, chlorophyll, and blue skate liver oil.

Change Your Diet

Making some additional dietary changes can greatly help to open your third eye. Some of the best things to include and implement into your diet are: raw cacao, goji berries, garlic, cilantro, lemons/limes, watermelon, bananas, honey, coconut oil, hemp seeds, seaweed, and noni juice!

All of those foods have detoxing properties which will help to nourish your body and improve the health of your pineal gland. Raw apple cider vinegar is another great food to add. Try drinking it with purified water and raw honey.

Use Essential Oils

Many essential oils can be used to stimulate the third eye, while also relaxing the body and mind, and reducing stress levels. Good choices include lavender, sandalwood, frankincense, parsley, davana, pine, pink lotus, and mugwort.

Be careful though to use your essential oils correctly! You should not inhale all of them directly, or put them directly on the skin without diluting them first. Each oil requires different method of use. You can burn them in a diffuser or add a few drops to bath water to begin with!

Sungazing

Gazing at the sun during sunrise and also sunset is believed to boost the proficiency of the Pineal gland, which will allow you greater control of your third eye!

Meditation

Meditation helps you to become one with your body, and gain greater control of your third eye. It is also said to help activate your chakras and unblock any chakras and energy paths which is vital to unleashing the power of your third eye!

Chanting

Chanting goes hand in hand with meditation. Chanting causes the tetrahedron bone in your nose to vibrate, which in turn stimulates the pineal gland.

The sound 'OM' resonates with the fourth chakra which opens you up to universal and cosmic awareness. Activating this 4th chakras opens up the chakras and allows energy to further travel up to the 6th chakra where the third eye resides.

Use Crystals

Crystals can be used for a variety of healing purposes and can also be used to enhance certain psychic abilities.

There are however, specific crystals that you can use to target the pineal gland. They include: amethyst, laser quartz, moonstone, pietersite, purple sapphire, purple violet tourmaline, rhodonite, rose aura, and sodalite.

Do however make sure that you are wary of what color crystals you are using. Any indigo, violet, or dark purple gemstone or crystal can be used to stimulate the pineal gland.

The most common way to use crystals to open your third eye are to place the crystal between your brow. They can also be held during meditation, and chanting.

A useful way to use crystals is to take an amethyst obelisk wand

Magnet Massage

Another method for decalcifying the pineal gland and awakening your third eye is to use a magnet. The common method involves attaching a magnet using an adhesive backing to the area just above your third eye.

Magnets have the ability to alkilise the body, and will help to decalcify the pineal gland.

This should be done for 2-3 hours at a time, and during waking hours. The sun will increase the performance of the magnet, so make sure you get outside for a while as you use it!

In Conclusion

All of the above methods have been shown to work. However, every single person in different!

For yourself, not all of these methods may produce the desired results. The best course of action is to choose multiple methods, and begin to test what feels right for you, and what is providing you with the best tangible results!

Chapter 6:
Chakras & The Third Eye

Chakras are the different energy points in your body that energy flows through. The belief of the Chakra system originates from India, and was first referenced to between 1500 and 500 BC in the oldest text called the 'Vedas'.

There are 7 primary Chakras that energy flows through in the body. The energy flow begins at the bottom with the first chakra, and flows up to the top of the body where the 7th Chakra is situated.

If there is a blockage in one of the Chakras, the energy will not continue to flow smoothly onward to the next Chakra. This can cause a range of spiritual, mental, and physical health problems. The Chakra responsible for the Third Eye is the 6th Chakra. Many people have blockages in their Chakras, which explains why so few people have the ability to use their Third Eye to it's full potential.

Below is a breakdown of the 7 primary Chakras and their functions.

Chakra 1 – Root Chakra

The Root Chakra represents our foundation. It provides us with a feeling of being grounded.

It is located at the very base of your spine, in the tailbone region.

It has emotional connections with issues such as: survival, financial stability, and the ability to access food. This Chakra in a way represents and is a reflection of our basic needs for survival.

When this Chakra is blocked or out of balance, greediness will be present. When it is clear and healthy, feelings of security, and a connection to the earth will be felt.

Chakra 2 – Sacral Chakra

The Sacral Chakra represents out connection to others and our ability to accept other people. It also represents our ability to accept new experiences.

It is located in the lower abdomen region, about 2 inches below the naval, and 2 inches in.

It has emotional connections with issues such as: a sense of abundance, our well-being, pleasure, and sexuality.

When this Chakra is blocked or out of balance, jealousy, anger, and codependency can be present. When it is clear and healthy, feelings of creativity and love will be felt.

Chakra 3 – Solar Plexus Chakra

The Solar Plexus Chakra represents our ability to be confident, and in control of ourselves and our lives.

It is located in the upper-abdomen, in the stomach region.

It has emotional connections with issues such as: self-worth, self-confidence, and self-esteem.

When this Chakra is blocked or out of balance, fear, guilt, and intimidation will be present. When it is clear and healthy, feelings of trust, self-esteem, confidence, and responsibility may be felt.

Chakra 4 – Heart Chakra

The Heart Chakra represents our ability to love.

It is located in the center of the chest, just above the heart.

It has emotional connections with issues such as: love, our ability to be loved and receive love, happiness, and inner peace.

When this Chakra is blocked or out of balance, resentment, hate, and loneliness may be present. When it is clear and healthy, feelings of peace, love, and connection to other/the environment may be felt.

Chakra 5 – Throat Chakra

The Throat Chakra represents our ability to communicate.

It is located in the middle of the throat.

It has emotional connections with issues such as: communication, our ability to express ourselves, our feelings, and the truth.

When this Chakra is blocked or out of balance, resentment, criticism, and addiction may be present. When it is clear and healthy, feelings of being balanced, the ability to easily express oneself, and the power of choice may be felt.

Chakra 6 – Third Eye Chakra (Also called the 'Brow Chakra')

The Third Eye Chakra represents our ability to see the big picture.

It is located between the eyes.

It has emotional connections with issues such as: imagination, intuition, wisdom, knowledge, and the ability to be decisive and have constructive thoughts.

When this Chakra is blocked or out of balance, learning difficulties or a tendency to lie may be present. When it is clear and healthy, feelings of great intuition may exist.

Chakra 7 – Crown Chakra

The Crown Chakra represents our ability to be fully connected spiritually.

It is located at the very top of the head.

It has emotional connections with issues such as: our beauty both inside and out, our connection to spirituality, and pure peace.

When this Chakra is blocked or out of balance, genetic disorders and selfishness may be present. When it is clear and healthy, feelings of being spiritually connected, and being at peace with God and the world may be felt.

As previously mentioned, the energy flows through our bodies beginning at the root chakra, all the way up to the crown chakra. Blockages along the way will halt the energy flow. The vast majority of people have blockages and cannot awaken their third eye because of it.

Even fewer ever are able to use their 7th chakra to it's full potential. People such as monks and shamans who make use of heavy meditation are most commonly associated with this chakra.

How to Unblock & Heal Your Chakras

In order to activate the Third Eye, we must first unblock and heal any issues in the Chakras below it.

You first need to analyze the list of the Chakras, and see if you have any symptoms of that Chakra being blocked. Start with the first Chakra and then work your way upwards.

Be honest with yourself about what issues may be present that are causing that particular blockage.

The best way to unblock and heal your Chakras begins with introspection. You must first be honest with yourself and identify that you have an emotional issue/s related to one (or more) of the Chakras. You then must delve deeper into the issue, and really understand why that it is occurring.

This can be quite a painful experience and it can bring up bad memories, but it is a necessary part of the process. You must be able to understand the emotional issues that at present (and we all have them), be able to accept them for what they are, and make a conscious effort to move on from them in a positive direction.

Chakra blockages can be for a short period of time, or for an extended period. They are commonly caused by emotional issues, but can also be caused by personality traits, and physical ailments/intoxication. Further, they can be blocked by a simple lack of use.

Identifying any emotional issues or personality traits that may be negatively affecting the Chakras, and making an effort to move on from them, is a great first step. However, this is often not enough. Most people have forgotten their ability to control the energy in their body, and this must be re-learned.

The greatest way to do this is through focus and meditation.

A common method is to do what is known as 'energy breathing'. In this exercise you focus on your breath in a meditative state, and visualize the breath as glowing energy. You need to imagine this energy entering your body, and moving through each of the Chakras, starting at the bottom and rising up to the top. Feel and focus on the sensation of the energy as it touches and activates each of your Chakras, flowing smoothly on to the next. Feel yourself let go of any emotional issues that relate to the particular Chakra as your direct your energy to it.

Many people prefer to perform this exercise outdoors in nature, as it provides a greater connection to the earth and gets you away from any external distractions.

Different people use a multitude of modalities to unlock, unblock, and heal the different Chakras. Some people use meditation, some people use therapy and introspection, some use chanting, and some use crystals. All methods have their merits, but the best course of action is to begin by identifying the blockage in the first place, and why it has occurred.

Overcoming the issues surrounding the occurrence of said blockage will help tremendously in healing your Chakras, and as a result, in your overall emotional wellbeing also.

The use of crystals with relation to the Third Eye will be discussed in the next chapter!

Chapter 7:
Using Crystals With Your Third Eye

Many people have used crystals throughout the world for thousands of years, for a variety of different purposes. Most commonly, they are used for healing. Certain crystals can be used for enhancing psychic abilities, by healing and strengthening the third eye.

This chapter will discuss the different crystals you might like to use, and how to use them to improve the health and function of your third eye.

Crystals For The Third Eye

There are several different crystals that work well with the third eye. I have listed the best ones you might want to use below:

- Clear Quartz: This crystal is often referred to as a 'master healer' due to its many different applications. It works to enhance, and clear all of your chakras, and can assist in focus and enhancing energy.

- Lapis Lazuli: This dark blue crystal is glittered with specks of gold. It works to connect you with spiritual vibrations, improving your psychic abilities.

- Labradorite: This is a protective stone which will keep you safe from negative energies and influences, whilst also strengthening your psychic abilities. Labradorite will protect you from taking on too much of other people's burdens, and will allow you to avoid too much stress.

- Amethyst: This crystal is often referred to as 'the stone of spirituality'. Amethyst can lift us to another level in our spiritual development, and is particularly helpful when trying to astral travel. It protects from negative dreams, and assists with improving your patience.

- Moonstone: This mystical stone can help you to awaken dormant psychic abilities. The abilities you have inside of you can be accessed once you have awakened your third eye, and this stone helps to achieve exactly that! This stone absorbs the power of the moon, so be sure to 'charge' it by occasionally leaving it in direct moonlight for a few hours.

How To Use Crystals

So, you now have a list of powerful crystals, but how do you actually use them? Well, there are a few different methods:

- Wear them: Crystals can be used simply by being worn. This can be in the form of a necklace, bracelet, earrings, or any other type of jewelry. It is ideal however for the crystal to be making direct contact with your skin.

- Carry them with you: If you don't want to wear your crystals as jewelry, that's okay – they can also be simply carried with you. Keep them in your pocket, in a special bag that you carry, or simply hold them in your hand.

- Sleep with them: Having crystals under your pillow, or directly next to your bed can be beneficial also. Particularly with crystals such as moonstone that assist with dreaming and astral travel, having them nearby during the night is very beneficial.

Chapter 8:
Ways To Sharpen Your Psychic Abilities

There are several ways to practice and develop your psychic abilities further. In this chapter a few of the best methods are provided for you to try out for yourself!

Psychic Development Practices to Start with:

These are simply meant to point you in the right direction. Please feel free to combine any of the following exercises, or even to invent your own. This is meant to be inspiring and fun, so add your own personal twist to it for optimal results.

- **Scanning Energy:** This technique can be practiced with a relative or friend. Stand about five feet from them, both closing your eyes. Breathe deeply for a few minutes to get grounded, and then attempt to visualize them as a beam of energy, rather than solid or material. Pay attention to any symbols, numbers, words, or thoughts that come into your mind, including patterns or colors. Once a couple of minutes has passed, and you regain consciousness, tell your partner your thoughts and ideas, and listen to theirs.

- **Using your Skills of Prediction:** This art is one method for gauging how far you've come with your psychic skills. You can begin this in a simple way, next time your cellphone rings, pause and focus your attention on the call, and who you believe is trying to reach you. Another method you can use is trying to take the temperature of a room, sensing any emotions that are within it. This could be happiness, tenseness, or excitement. Focus in on the people in the room and try to see what they are feeling.

- Once you get into a habit of doing this, it will come automatically and your thoughts will come easily to you. You can confirm whether your feelings are correct or not by what transpires later on in that room. When you predicted that the temperature of the room was tense, did an argument break out? When you sensed happiness in the room, was the conversation positive and joyful?

- **Object Sensing:** Begin with items or objects that familiar people own. This is the best way to begin because once you have a feeling or thought toward the object, you can confirm whether or not it was correct. You can do this by holding an item and paying attention to any ideas or visions that appear in your mind, including scents or feelings. Since every item holds vibrations of history inside of it, these can be seen by you. Take some time to reflect on what you have picked up before sharing it with someone else. When you're ready, they can either confirm or deny your feelings.

- **Premonitions:** Every person out there has ideas of what will come, premonitions, or visions, that haven't occurred yet. This is because our minds are constantly sensing what is in this world and universe, although we may not realize that that is what's happening. Writing down these feelings can help you notice when your visions are correct. You can then notice when they happen or when they don't. When you start to pay attention to them, you can verify their reality or truth, but if you never pay attention, you will miss them altogether.

- **Noticing Impressions in the Mind:** Each morning, before getting caught up in your daily routine, pause to have some quiet time, and then ask the question "What will happen today?" Include details about how you will feel, who you will see, and any other details that come to you. Don't write off any impressions, because you can't know what is correct before giving it a chance. Once your day has ended, go over this list to see what you were correct about.

- **Meditation:** This should be done each and every day, for a minimum of 10 minutes each session. When you wish to develop your skills in the psychic realm, you have to raise your energy and vibration, since the energy of spirit is always at a frequency that is higher. To access this, and thus gain psychic benefits from it, meditation can be used. This state allows you to raise your vibration at will, as you enter a relaxed state of being. You will then be more connected to energy, yours, that of others, and that of the divine spirit.

- **Getting in Touch with Spirit Guides:** When you mediate, you can take this opportunity to meet your guides. As soon as you enter the relaxed state completely, request for your spirit guide or guides to make themselves known. Try to find out what their names are, and don't hold back on saying what you feel you should say. Have trust in the process, and allow your intuition to guide you.

- **Notice your Dreams:** In order to hone your psychic abilities, you should notice what your dreams are telling you. Notice the images coming through in your dreams, especially symbols that repeat themselves. There is a reason why these messages are coming through, so you should treat them with respect.

- **Practice Energy Readings on Objects:** This is a fun way to test your skills and practice your psychic abilities. You just need to place an object into your hands, or simply touch it. This should be something made of metal that has a lot of history or emotion attached to it, such as a sentimentally valuable piece of jewelry. Once you've done this, hold the object for a while and allow any information that may be there to come through to you, including names and emotions. Again this is best done with the object of someone you are familiar with, so you can confirm if your intuitions are correct.

- **Object Visualization:** You can improve your skills of clairvoyance using visualization. This is best done with natural objects, such as a stone or flower. Focus your attention completely on every detail of the object. This is meant to strengthen your powers of observation and get you in the habit of noticing detail, which will then translate over to your mental and psychic life.

- **General Visualization:** This is similar to the step above, but no specific object is necessary, and this can be entirely random. It's best to take on this step after you have already mastered the object visualization exercise. To do this method, get into a relaxed state, with your eyes closed, and place your attention on your brow, where your third eye is located. Ask for your guide to give you a peaceful and beautiful image to look at, and allow as many images to come through as you can. Try not to think too much, and instead allow your mind to rest without words.

- **Get Acquainted with Nature**: Taking a walk outside can help you get in touch with your latent psychic skills. You can even do a walking meditation out among the trees, focusing in on each step as you go, clearing your head and raising your energy levels. Since attaining psychic skills is more about clearing out the clutter that is standing in the way than anything else, this is a great way to do so.

- **Immerse yourself in Related Writing**: The best way to get in the flow of any new path is to read and think about it often. There are plenty of valuable resources out there on this subject, to be found on the internet or in your local library. Also the simple act of focusing on this subject will help you stay in the zone.

- **Go to Antique Shops**: Next time you visit a shop full of old stuff, pay attention to how you're feeling when you're there. Browse the store and pick up some items, noticing whether anything comes to you, such as a vision, a name, or anything else. This is great practice for a developing psychic, since these old objects will have existing memories and histories within each of them.

- **Keep a Psychic Development Journal**: This is an important step. Information from the realm beyond can come to you in many different ways, and oftentimes is meant to be metaphorical or symbolic. Since this information seems to appear to you at random, it can be hard to make sense of it all, which is where recording your findings down in a journal comes in. Your guide is there to help you both notice and interpret the data that comes through to you. Not only will this allow you to record your progress, but you can also review it in a few months to see how far you've come on your journey.

- It's easy to lose track of how much progress we're making until we see proof of where we once were, and journal entries can be great for this reason. At the end of the day, review each sentence you wrote to see if you notice any patterns emerging or other relevant information. Write everything down, however seemingly insignificant, because it may make sense later.

- Writing is a key way to stay in touch with your higher or divine self, which is responsible for your psychic gifts. Don't forgo this valuable chance to connect with that part of you.

- **Research related Material:** This can include chakras and auras. Seeing auras is another psychic skill that anyone can do. You can practice this on yourself or a friend. Make sure that there is a solid wall behind your friend or you, and try to focus on the space that surrounds the body. After a while, you should notice that the air is shimmering in this area. As you practice this skill more and more, you may start to notice colors.

- **Practice Hearing beyond:** Part of developing your psychic skills is paying attention to what you would have previously ignored or not seen as significant. When you are falling asleep at night, sit quietly and pay attention to every sound you can hear. Paying attention to these noises, which you might not regularly notice, will help you strengthen your gift of hearing, both of this world and beyond.

- **Give Readings**: If you wish to develop your psychic abilities or even become a medium, this is a key step. It's just like developing any other skill; the more you practice it, the better you get. Find some interested or willing friends and put your skills to the test. If it doesn't go the way you wished it would, at first, don't worry, it's normal to take a while to get good at this, and it will come with time and dedication.

- **Look at Old Pictures**: Look through some of your family's old pictures and see if you can notice anything about relatives you've never known. This can be a great way to test your instincts, because you can confirm your findings with a living relative who did know the deceased family member, to see if you were right.

- **Find Likeminded Friends:** It helps a lot to have friends with similar interests as you, when exploring a new skill. Join a circle or class about becoming psychic, which will allow you access to likeminded people. You can then practice your skills with them, and they can practice theirs with you. Getting to know other mediums or aspiring psychics is an interesting pursuit.

- **Practice Turning on and off your Abilities**: When you begin to follow this path, it's important to figure out how to control your skills. When your abilities are turned on constantly, you are in danger of absorbing energies that you shouldn't absorb. Doing a positivity meditation and then asking your guide to protect you should suffice for this. You also need to know how to shut the skills off when you need to. You can do this by thanking your guide for helping you, and saying goodbye.

Chapter 9:
Third Eye Awakening With Meditation

As briefly mentioned in the previous chapter, meditation can be a powerful way to enhance your psychic abilities, and awaken your third eye.

Some people believe that meditation alone can in fact, open the third eye.

Meditation is similar to a muscle, and you must train it regularly to improve your abilities, and reach deeper states of meditation. I would recommend meditating every single day, for a minimum of 10 minutes. Ideally, the longer that you practice for, the better!

In this chapter I will share with you a type of meditation known as 'Trataka'. This form of meditation is specifically for the third eye.

To properly perform the Trataka meditation, follow the steps below:

1. Sit in the lotus pose (with your legs crossed)

2. Keep your spine straight

3. Close your eyes

4. Inhale and exhale deeply 3 times

5. Concentrate on the middle of your forehead on the third eye area

6. With your eyes closed, move your eyes to point towards this third eye area. If your eyes were open, you would be cross-eyed and looking upwards

7. Begin slowly counting backwards from 100, keeping your eyes centered on the third eye

8. By the time you have finished counting backwards, you should feel a still state of calm

9. Continue to keep your eyes focused on the third eye for 10-15 minutes, staying still and keeping your mind quiet. Simply focus on the third eye and how it feels

10. Slowly shift your eyes back to a normal position and be still for a few minutes

11. Open your eyes

12. Remain in the lotus pose for a few minutes, inhaling and exhaling deeply

For optimal benefits, it's recommended that you perform this meditation both in the morning and during the evening. As mentioned throughout this book, awakening the third eye can sometimes be a long and arduous process. It can take some time to become proficient at meditation, but do not be discouraged!

After consistently performing this meditation for a few weeks, your meditation skills will have greatly improved, and consequently so will have your psychic abilities!

Chapter 10:
Third Eye Awakening With Health & Diet

Your diet can greatly affect the health of your third eye, and how easily you're able to awaken it.

The modern day American diet is full of processed foods, chemicals, additives, and is devoid of a lot of the nutrients that our bodies need.

In order to keep your body both physically and spiritually healthy, it is absolutely vital that you are careful of what you put into it!

Foods You Should Consume

Here is a list of some foods that you should consume. These will help to improve the health of your third eye, and de-calcify it:

- Green Vegetables
- Fruit
- Non-Processed Juices
- Organic Food
- Grass-Fed Meats
- Nuts
- Healthy Oils such as Coconut and Olive Oil

Foods To Avoid

Just as important as the foods that you should consume, are the ones that you should avoid. Not only can these physically effect you, they can also have negative effects on the third eye. The most important of these to avoid is fluoride, as it is the main culprit in calcifying the third eye! Here is a list of what you should be avoiding in your diet:

- Processed Foods
- All Junk Food
- High Fructose Corn Syrup
- Genetically Modified Fruit & Vegetables
- Non-Organic Meats
- Tap Water (if fluoride is added)
- Toothpaste (with fluoride added)

Chapter 11:
The Pineal Gland & DMT

The Pineal Gland

The Pineal gland is a small, rice-sized gland situated in-between our brows, in the position of the third eye. This gland is an endocrine gland, responsible for producing melatonin, a hormone derived from tryptophan, which plays a major role in the regulation of our circadian rhythm.

Melatonin also helps in the development of the reproductive system, and inhibits the production of certain hormones produced by the pituitary gland.

The Pineal gland is shaped like a pine-cone, but when dissected resembles an eye.

Many people and cultures consider the Pineal gland and the third eye to be one and the same. They believe that it is the physical gland responsible for psychic abilities.

Unlike the majority of the human brain, the Pineal gland is not isolated from the body by the blood-brain barrier. In fact, it has incredible blood flow, second only to the kidney!

The gland continues to grow until 1-2 years of age, and stops when it reaches 5-8mm. Once puberty hits, the gland often grows further.

Calcification of the Gland

It has been discovered that when fluoride is present in a person's diet, it concentrates extremely heavily in the Pineal gland, having a negative effect upon it.

This concentration of fluoride can cause the pineal gland to calcify. The fluoride gathers in the Pineal gland, forming phosphate crystals. This hardens the gland and lowers its function, meaning less melatonin is produced and the circadian rhythm is affected.

The calcification of the Pineal gland has also been linked to the early onset of puberty, and a presence of abnormal hormonal triggers.

Foods that can specifically help to de-calcify and strengthen this gland include:

- Cacao
- Beans
- Turmeric
- Green Vegetables
- Grass Juices
- Spring Water
- Reishi Mushroom Tea
- Beets
- Apple Cider Vinegar

DMT

DMT or dimethyltryptamine, otherwise known as 'the dream molecule' is also produced by the pineal gland.

DMT is produced when we sleep, and is commonly attributed to causing our dreams to occur.

DMT is the primary component of ayahuasca, an Amazonian drink that causes the user to enter an incredible dream world for a short period of time. Many people during these trips claim to see a woman commonly referred to as 'Mother Ayahuasca', and she teaches them important lessons. These experiences are often life-changing, and help people to find clarity in their lives.

The amount of DMT in ayahuasca is a much larger amount than what our Pineal glands can produce, and thus, the results are dramatic. The journey provides people with a lot of clarity, and they often see a spirit guide type of figure who guides them in the right direction.

By having a healthy pineal gland, our bodies are able to produce DMT more easily. This enhances our psychic abilities, and allows us to have more of these DMT fueled experiences.

Many people believe that DMT is the key to us activating our psychic abilities, and finding the world beyond. Ensure that your Pineal gland is in good health, and you will have the best chance of improving your psychic abilities.

Chapter 12: How To Avoid Pineal Gland Calcification

As mentioned in the previous chapter, avoiding calcification of the Pineal gland is highly important. This chapter will summarize a few of the steps you can take to avoid Pineal gland calcification, or to assist in de-calcifying the gland.

Avoid These Foods

Do not consume any of the following:

- Processed Foods
- Fluoride
- High Fructose Corn Syrup
- Chemical Additives
- Artificial Colors & Flavors
- Genetically Modified Foods

Consume These Foods

Increase the quantities you consume of these foods:

- Organic Fruits & Vegetables
- Grass Juices
- Cacao

- Beans
- Turmeric
- Apple Cider Vinegar
- Pink Himalayan Salt
- Beets
- Reishi Mushroom Tea
- Spring Water

In addition to avoiding certain foods and consuming others, it is also important to stay active. Your physical activity doesn't have to be intense, just make sure that you stay moving. Going for a long walk each day, or doing yoga is highly recommended.

Meditating is also very beneficial to the Pineal gland. Try and perform the meditation we covered earlier at least once per day.

Finally, vitamin D is very important. Make sure that you get plenty of direct sunlight throughout the day, or take a vitamin D supplement for best results.

Chapter 13:
The Third Eye & Brainwave Levels

When you are in a deep meditative state, your brain enters a state known as 'Theta'. This level of brainwave activity is when your third eye is most powerful, and where you will have the best access to your psychic abilities.

Humans have 5 different types of brainwaves, or electrical patterns. The 5 types are:

- Gamma

- Beta

- Alpha

- Theta

- Delta

Each different level of brainwave activity has its purpose, but for third eye awakening and tapping into psychic abilities, Theta is best. Our bodies ability to switch through different brain wave types greatly determines how we handle stress, cope with various situations, and how quickly and effectively we can begin to use our psychic prowess.

There are a couple of ways to get into a Theta state.

The first method is once again, through meditation! As you get better at meditation and can reach deeper and deeper states, this will become easier.

At first, it is normal to dip in and out of a Theta state. As you practice and progress however, it will become easier to reach the state, and also to stay in it for longer with less effort! Getting into a Theta state through meditation is a great thing to do prior to practicing your psychic abilities.

The second method for reaching a Theta state is using a technological aid. This is usually an audio track, designed to slow your mind. It will automatically guide your brain to relax it deeper, and deeper. These audio tracks are made of certain frequencies that can have profound effect on your brainwave activity. Examples of these audio tracks can be found on YouTube.

When you reach a Theta brainwave level, the left and right hemispheres of your brain will be able to communicate. This helps in activating your third eye, provides you with clarity, relaxation, and a sense of calm.

In this state, you will be able to develop your psychic abilities much faster, gain more control over the power of your third eye, and train it to stay awakened!

Conclusion

Thanks again for taking the time to read through this book!

You should now have a good understanding the third eye, and be well on your way to awakening its power, and unlocking all of your psychic abilities!

If you enjoyed this book, please take the time to leave me a review on Amazon. I appreciate your honest feedback, and it really helps me to continue producing high quality books.

Printed in the USA
CPSIA information can be obtained
at www.ICGtesting.com
LVHW010938170224
772110LV00003B/31